OLSAT® PRACTICE TEST - LEVEL C

OLSAT® Practice Test - Level C

Written and published by: Bright Kids NYC

Copyright © 2013 by Bright Kids NYC Inc. All of the questions in this book have been created by the staff and consultants of Bright Kids NYC Inc.

The *Otis-Lennon School Ability Test®* (OLSAT®) is a registered trademark of NCS Pearson Inc. Pearson Inc. neither endorses nor supports the content of the Bright Kids NYC OLSAT® Practice Test for Second Grade – Level C.

All rights reserved. No part of this book may be reproduced or transmitted in any form or by any means without written permission from the author. ISBN (978-1-935858-90-4)

Bright Kids NYC Inc.
www.brightkidsnyc.com
info@brightkidsnyc.com
917-539-4575

OLSAT® PRACTICE TEST - LEVEL C

About Bright Kids NYC 5

Introduction 7

OLSAT® Overview 9

Content 11

OLSAT® Level C Structure 13

Scoring Guidelines 15

General Administration Guidelines 17

Getting Ready 19

Instructions 21

    Part 1 25

    Part 2 27

    Part 3 29

Answer Key 37

Student's Booklet 41

About Bright Kids NYC

Bright Kids NYC was founded in New York City to provide language arts and math enrichment for young children. Our goal is to prepare students of all ages for standardized exams through assessments, tutoring workshops, and our publications. Our philosophy is that, regardless of age, test taking is a skill that can be acquired and mastered through practice.

At Bright Kids NYC, we strive to provide the best learning materials. Our publications are truly unique. All of our books have been created by qualified psychologists, learning specialists, teachers, and staff writers. Our books have also been tested by hundreds of children in our tutoring practice. Since children can make associations that many adults cannot, testing of materials by children is a critical step towards creating successful test preparation guides. Finally, our learning specialists, teaching staff, and writers have provided practical strategies and tips to help students compete successfully on standardized exams.

Feel free to contact us if you have any questions.

Bright Kids NYC Inc. Corporate Headquarters
225 Broadway
Suite 1400
New York, New York 10007

Phone: 917-539-4575
Email: info@brightkidsnyc.com
www.brightkidsnyc.com

Introduction

Bright Kids NYC created the OLSAT® Practice Tests to familiarize students with the content and format of the OLSAT®. Students, no matter how bright they may be, do not always perform well if they are not accustomed to the format and structure of a standardized exam. They can misunderstand the directions or fail to carefully read a question and properly consider all of the answer choices. Thus, without adequate preparation and familiarization, a student may not perform to the best of his or her ability on a standardized exam like the OLSAT®.

The Bright Kids OLSAT® Level C Practice Test can be used as a diagnostic tool to help assess a student's ability to perform well on the various sections of the actual exam. If you have purchased our OLSAT® Preparation Guide, you can use the practice test in this book to see how well your child performs on a simulated OLSAT®. The OLSAT® Level C Test is typically given to children in Second Grade.

The Bright Kids OLSAT® Level C Practice Test is not designed to generate a score or a percentile rank since the test has not been standardized with actual OLSAT® norms and measures. The objectives of the practice test are to identify a student's strengths, weaknesses, and overall test-taking ability in order to adequately prepare him or her for the actual exam. Our answer key lists the type of every test question in this book. You should use the answer key to easily identify the types of OLSAT® questions your child finds difficult to solve.

In order to maximize the effectiveness of the Bright Kids OLSAT® Practice Test, it is important to first familiarize yourself with the test and its instructions. In addition, it is recommended that you work with your child in a neutral environment free of noise and clutter. Finally, a comfortable seating arrangement may help the child focus and concentrate to the best of his or her ability.

Most students will have to take numerous standardized exams throughout their school years. The best way to develop the critical thinking skills needed for these types of exams is to practice with similarly-styled exams under test-like conditions. This method helps ensure that a student will succeed on his or her exam.

OLSAT® Overview

The *Otis Group Intelligence Scale* was created and published by Dr. Arthur Otis at Stanford University in 1918. The *Otis Group Intelligence Scale* was followed by the *Otis Self-Administering Tests of Mental Ability*, the *Otis Quick-Scoring Mental Ability Tests*, the *Otis-Lennon Mental Ability Test*, and finally the *Otis-Lennon School Ability Test* (OLSAT®). The purpose of the exam is to assess a student's aptitude for in-school performance by testing his or her cognitive and reasoning abilities.

The *Otis-Lennon School Ability Test*® Eighth Edition (OLSAT® 8) is currently administered in various education programs in New York, Connecticut, California, Texas, and Virginia. Some of these programs are described below.

New York City Gifted and Talented programs administer the OLSAT® for entry into District and Citywide Gifted and Talented programs. The OLSAT® is administered in connection with the *Naglieri Nonverbal Ability Test*® (NNAT®2). Currently, students are required to perform at or above the 90th percentile rank to be eligible for the district programs and at or above the 97th percentile to be eligible for the citywide programs. Additional information can be found at http://schools.nyc.gov/Academics/GiftedandTalented. In NYC, the level C test is given in 2nd Grade for 3rd Grade entry.

The Davis Unified School District in California uses the OLSAT® for students in Grades 3-8 to qualify for entry into the District Gifted and Talented programs. Students must receive a total OLSAT® score of 96% or higher and a Verbal or Nonverbal score in the 96th percentile or higher to qualify for the Gifted and Talented Education programs (GATE).

The Greenwich Public Schools District Board of Education uses the OLSAT®, in conjunction with the *Stanford Achievement Test* Series, to evaluate students in the 3rd, 5th, and 7th grades. Each student's OLSAT® score helps predict his or her performance on the *Stanford Achievement Test* and enables the District to compare achievement scores. The OLSAT® is also used to predict performance on the *Connecticut Mastery Test*, a mandated year-end exam.

Content

In order to succeed on the OLSAT®, students must accurately perceive pattern relationships and recall what has been perceived. Students also need to use their reasoning abilities to comprehend abstract items and to apply generalizations to new and different contexts. These reasoning abilities are measured through the student's performance on verbal and nonverbal questions.

Verbal Questions

Verbal questions are centered on a student's ability to listen carefully, follow directions, and understand vocabulary through receptive language. While verbal questions do require verbal knowledge, all multiple-choice options are given in a visual format. A student must listen closely to what the administrator says, make logical inferences from the information he or she has been given, and use his or her academic skills and knowledge of the world to select the correct answer.

There are three types of questions that are used to test a student's verbal skills

1) **Following Directions:** Following Directions questions assess a student's ability to select the correct visual representation that corresponds to the verbal description that was read out loud. Students are asked to apply relational concepts when finding the correct answer to pictorial and figural representations.

2) **Aural Reasoning:** Aural Reasoning questions test the student's ability to visualize a certain scenario, integrate appropriate details, make logical inferences, and synthesize what has been described. Students are asked to understand details, main ideas, and to predict the outcomes of situations.

3) **Arithmetic Reasoning:** Arithmetic Reasoning incorporates number reasoning into the solving of verbal problems. These questions test basic mathematical reasoning concepts such as counting, quantity, estimation, and inequalities. This section also has spoken word problems that employ addition, subtraction, and simple fractions to test the student's complex reasoning skills.

Nonverbal Questions

Nonverbal questions focus on a child's visual, spatial, and arithmetic understandings. Unlike the verbal questions, no verbal background knowledge is needed in this section. These nonverbal questions highlight reasoning skills that are independent of language (with the exception of the test directions which give the student verbal instructions on how to complete the tasks).

There are four types of questions that are used to test a student's nonverbal skills:

1) **Analogies:** An analogy is defined as the comparison of a similarity between two different things. Analogical reasoning is the ability to use parallel cases to draw a conclusion. For students, analogical reasoning on the OLSAT® is assessed through pictures or figural elements. Analogy questions require a student to infer a relationship between the first two items and then select an item that completes the second relationship in the same manner.

2) **Classifications:** Classification questions require students to figure out what does not belong among a group of items. All but one of the pictures or figures in each question share a minimum of one common trait or characteristic. The student must evaluate the similarities and differences between each picture in order to find the correct answer. Classifications can be figural or pictorial.

3) **Figural Series:** Figural Series questions assess a student's ability to evaluate a sequential series of geometric shapes and then predict the next occurrence, or "what comes next", in the series.

4) **Pattern Matrix:** Pattern Matrix questions evaluate the student's ability to find the next step in a geometric series based on a set of rules. Students need to identify the rules and then predict the geometric shape that belongs in place of the question mark in the matrix.

OLSAT® Level C Structure

The OLSAT® is a multiple-choice test. It is not necessary for a student to read or write to take the Level C test. The Level C test is administered in a group setting and students are required to mark their answers by filling in the corresponding answer bubble. The content and structure of the OLSAT® varies for each grade level. The Level C test is given to Second Grade students and contains 60 questions that assess a student's verbal and nonverbal reasoning skills.

TABLE 1: Distribution of Types of Questions[1]

Types of Questions	Number of Questions
VERBAL	**30**
Following Directions	12
Aural Reasoning	12
Arithmetic Reasoning	6
NONVERBAL	**30**
Picture Classification	5
Figural Classification	7
Picture Analogies	5
Figural Analogies	7
Figural Series	3
Pattern Matrix	3
Total	**60**

[1] This chart may not reflect the exact distribution of questions on the actual exam since the mix between verbal and nonverbal questions and among different types of questions varies from year to year.

Scoring Guidelines

The results of the OLSAT® comprise a wealth of useful information for test users. Derived scores based on age and grade comparisons can be provided for verbal, nonverbal, and total raw scores. Raw scores, which are defined as the number of questions answered correctly, do not provide enough information to properly assess the quality of a student's performance. However, a scaled score system connects all test levels and yields a continuous scale that can be used to compare the performances of students taking different levels of the same content cluster. Scaled scores are particularly useful for evaluating changes in performance over time and for out-of-level testing. Scaled scores can also be translated into percentile ranks. For example, New York City Gifted and Talented programs only provide percentile ranks and composite scores while other districts in the United States provide more detailed information.

Since the test changes from year to year, the number of questions a student must answer correctly to obtain a specific scaled score will vary based on that particular test's curve and distribution. OLSAT® scores also take into account the age of the student. The test is normed in three-month age bands; students who are younger can miss more questions and still get the same percentile rank and scaled score as older students who are within the same grade.

The Bright Kids OLSAT® Level C Practice Test can only be scored by the total number of correct answers. Please realize that a student can miss many questions on the actual test and still obtain a high score. Since this practice test has not been standardized with the OLSAT®, scaled scores or percentile ranks cannot be obtained from the raw score. Thus, the Bright Kids OLSAT® Level C Practice Test should be utilized as a learning tool to help evaluate a student's strengths and weaknesses on various question types rather than predict what his or her scaled score or percentile rank will be on the actual exam.

General Admnistration Guidelines

The Level C test is typically administered in three parts and in one sitting. There is a five-minute recommended rest period between Parts 1 and 2 and two rest periods in Part 3. The test pace in Part 3 is determined by the examiner, so there is no specific time limit for that part of the test. The time allocations below are given to provide an exact or approximate range of how much time may be needed to complete each part of the test. The recommended timeline is as follows:

Part 1: Examples	Approximately 5 minutes
Part 1: Administration	6 minutes
Rest Period	**Approximately 5 minutes**
Part 2: Examples	Approximately 5 minutes
Part 2: Administration	6 minutes
Rest Period	**Approximately 5 minutes**
Part 3: Examples	Approximately 5 minutes
Part 3: Administration (items 25-39)	Approximately 10 minutes
Rest Period	**Approximately 5 minutes**
Part 3 Administration (items 40-60)	Approximately 15 minutes

Getting Ready

Materials

1) Remove the "Student's Booklet" section from this book and staple the pages in order.

2) Several No. 2 soft lead pencils, a soft eraser, and a pencil sharpener.

3) Ideally, a "Do Not Disturb" sign for the room where the test will be administered.

Prior to Testing

1) Familiarize yourself with the test and its instructions. You may want to take the test beforehand so that you can later explain to your child why certain answers are correct or incorrect.

2) Provide satisfactory physical conditions in the room where the test will be administered. Make sure there is ample lighting and ventilation in the room. Also, make sure that the table is free of clutter and that you and the child can both sit comfortably at the table together.

3) To prevent interruptions, administer the test when there are no other distractions in the house. If the house is not suitable, try to find a local library or school.

During Testing

1) Make sure that the child is comfortable marking down the answers. You may want to show him or her how to accurately fill in the bubbles on the sample questions.

2) Read all of the instructions exactly as they are written; do not paraphrase or change the questions.

3) Read each item only once. If there was a disturbance in the room that distracted the child, you may repeat the item.

4) Pace the test and utilize breaks as needed.

5) Do not give the child any feedback during testing unless otherwise instructed. Discuss the answers only after the completion of the test.

6) Provide positive reinforcements to ensure that the child completes the test. If he or she slows down or wants to give up, provide support and encouragement to help him or her finish the test.

Bright Kids NYC OLSAT® Practice Test

Instructions

Level C

Second Grade

No parts of this practice test may be reproduced or transmitted in any form or by any means without written permission from Bright Kids NYC Inc. ISBN (978-1-935858-90-4)

INSTRUCTIONS

Instructions

Please remember to detach and staple the section titled "Student's Booklet". Put the booklet in front of the child and instruct him or her to keep the booklet closed until you are both ready to begin. Make sure to have at least two sharpened pencils and a soft eraser on the testing table.

Reminder: **This practice test is designed to simulate the experience of taking an actual OLSAT®. The administrators of the OLSAT® are instructed to strictly follow the script. Therefore, it is important for you to follow the script exactly and to ask each question only once. The script has been bolded to help differentiate it from the rest of the directions.**

INSTRUCTIONS

Sample Questions and Test Administration

Part 1

Place the "Student's Booklet" in front of the child.

SAY: **Today, we are going to do some fun activities in the booklet in front of you.**

Sample A

SAY: **Now, open your booklet and look at the first page. Let's look at the first sample question. Here, you will see some pictures that go across. When pictures go across, they are said to be in a row. In this row, you see five items that people can use. One of these items does not belong with the other items. Find the item that is not like the other items.**

Pause while the child looks for the correct object.

SAY: **Which item did you find?**

Pause for a response.

SAY: **The first item is not like the other items. The other items are all used to cut things, but the fork is not an item used for cutting things. The fork is different from all of the other items.**

Make sure the child is comfortable with the answer to Sample A before proceeding.

SAY: **Since the fork is different from the other items, you should mark the circle under the picture of the fork. Color in the circle completely using your pencil. Try to fill in the circle as best as you can.**

Demonstrate how to fill in an answer if the child seems confused. If necessary, remind the child that he or she can only bubble in one answer choice. Then, proceed to Sample B.

Sample B

SAY: **Now, look at the figures in the second row. One of these figures does not belong with the other figures. Find the figure that is not like the other figures and mark under it.**

Pause while the child looks for the correct figure.

SAY: **Which figure did you mark?**

INSTRUCTIONS

Pause for a response.

SAY: **The fourth figure is different from the other figures. All of the other figures have a black circle that is next to a shaded piece of the circle. The fourth figure has a black circle that is in front of the shaded piece of the circle. Do you understand why the fourth figure is different from the other figures?**

Pause for a response. Make sure the child understands both examples before moving on to the practice test questions in Part 1.

SAY: **On the next few pages, you will be doing more activities like these. You will complete the rest of the problems in this section by marking under the picture or figure that is different from the other pictures or figures. You will have six minutes to complete this portion of the test. If you are having trouble with a problem, skip it and go on to the next problem. After you have answered question 12, you must STOP and not go any further in the test. You may go back and work on any questions that you have skipped in this section if you finish early, or you can go back and check your work in this section, but do not move ahead. Do you have any questions?**

Answer any questions the student may have before proceeding.

SAY: **Now you may begin working.**

Make sure that you begin timing as the student begins this section of the test. At the end of six minutes, the student must stop working on the first section of this test.

SAY: **Stop working and put your pencil down. We will now take a break.**

Administer a five-minute break. Make sure to tell the child that the test is not finished and that this is just a brief break.

INSTRUCTIONS

Part 2

Tell the child that it is time to come back and continue with the activities.

Sample C

SAY: **Now we are going to do a different activity. Turn to the next page in your booklet. Look at the first row. Here, you see four boxes. In the first box at the top, there is a whole pizza. In the box next to the whole pizza, there is a slice of pizza. These top two boxes go together in a certain way. Now, look at the first box on the bottom row where there is a loaf of bread. The other box next to the loaf of bread is empty. Now, look at the row of four pictures that is next to the four boxes. Which picture shows an item that goes with a loaf of bread in the same way that a slice of pizza goes with a whole pizza? Mark under that picture.**

Pause while the child looks for the correct picture.

SAY: **Which picture did you mark under?**

Pause for a response.

SAY: **The first picture is the correct answer. If a slice of pizza goes with a whole pizza, then a slice of bread goes with a whole loaf of bread. That's why the first picture belongs in the empty box. Do you understand why the first picture is the correct answer?**

Pause for a response. Make sure the child understands Sample C before moving on to Sample D.

Sample D

SAY: **Now, look at the second row. There are two figures in the top row of boxes. These two figures go together in a certain way. In the first box at the top, there is a white circle with three smaller black circles above it. In the second box at the top, the three black circles are now inside the white circle. Now, look at the figures inside the box on the bottom row. What do you think belongs in the empty box next to the figures? Mark under the figure that belongs in the empty box.**

Pause while the child looks for the correct answer.

SAY: **Which figure did you mark under?**

INSTRUCTIONS

Pause for a response.

SAY: **The second figure is the correct answer. The first row of boxes show that the smaller black shapes from the first box have moved into the larger white shape in the second box. The figure that belongs in the empty box should show that the small black shapes from the first box have moved into the large white shape. Thus, the figure that belongs in the empty box is a white triangle with three small black triangles inside of it. That's why the second figure is correct. Do you understand why the second figure is the correct answer?**

Pause for a response. Make sure the child understands all of the examples in this section before moving on to the practice test questions in Part 2.

SAY: **On the next few pages, you will be doing more activities like these. You will complete the rest of the problems in this section by marking under the picture or figure that belongs in the empty box. You will have six minutes to complete this portion of the test. If you are having trouble with a problem, skip it and go on to the next problem. After you have answered question 24, you must STOP and not go any further in the test. You may go back and work on any questions that you have skipped in this section if you finish early, or you can go back and check your work in this section, but do not move ahead. Do you have any questions?**

Answer any questions the student may have before proceeding.

SAY: **Now you may begin working.**

Make sure that you begin timing as the student begins this section of the test. At the end of six minutes, the student must stop working on the second section of this test.

SAY: **Stop working and put your pencil down. We will now take a break.**

Administer a five-minute break. Make sure to tell the child that the test is not finished and that this is just a brief break.

INSTRUCTIONS

Part 3

Tell the child that it is time to come back and continue with the activities.

Sample E

SAY: **Now we are going to do a different activity. Look at the first row at the top of the next page. Listen very carefully to what I say. John went to a farm and saw four cats. None of the cats looked exactly the same, and one of them was black. Mark under the picture that shows the cats John saw at the farm.**

Pause while the child looks for the correct picture.

SAY: **Which picture did you mark under?**

Pause for a response.

SAY: **The second picture is the correct answer. This picture shows four cats that all look different. One of the cats is also black. Do you understand why the second picture is the correct answer?**

Pause for a response. Make sure your child understands Sample E before moving on to Sample F.

Sample F

SAY: **Now, look at the next row. Mark under the picture that shows this: The largest jar is empty and the rest of the jars are full.**

Pause while the child looks for the correct picture.

SAY: **Which picture did you mark under?**

Pause for a response.

SAY: **The third picture is the correct answer. This is the only picture that shows a large empty jar and two smaller jars that are full. Do you understand why the third picture is the correct answer?**

Pause for a response. Make sure your child understands Sample F before moving on to Sample G.

INSTRUCTIONS

Sample G

SAY: **Turn to the next page and look at the top row of boxes. There is a figure in each box. These figures go together in a certain way as you move from left to right. Look at the group of figures to the right of the boxes. Mark under the figure that belongs in the empty box.**

Pause while the child looks for the correct figure.

SAY: **The third picture is the correct answer. In each box, the part of the circle that is black rotates clockwise to the next part of the circle. The figure that belongs in the empty box should have a black section in the lower left-hand corner of the circle. That figure is shown in the third answer choice. Do you understand why the third figure is the correct answer?**

Pause for a response. Make sure your child understands Sample G before moving on to Sample H.

Sample H

SAY: **Now, look at the next row. The figures inside the boxes go together in a certain way as you move from left to right. Look at the figures to the right of the boxes. Mark under the figure that belongs in the empty box.**

Pause while the child looks for the correct figure.

SAY: **Which figure did you mark under?**

Pause for a response.

SAY: **The third shape is the correct answer. In each row, as you move from left to right, the shape is rotating in a clockwise direction. The shape in the last row is a hexagon. In the first box, the left side of the hexagon is shaded and the hexagon is standing on one of its points. In the second box, the shape has been rotated clockwise so that the top half of the hexagon is now shaded and the hexagon is standing on one of its sides. The picture that belongs in the third box shows a hexagon that has been rotated clockwise again so that the right half of the hexagon is shaded and it is standing on one of its points. Do you understand why the third shape is the correct answer?**

Pause for a response. Make sure your child understands all of the examples in this section before moving on to the practice test questions in Part 3.

INSTRUCTIONS

SAY: On the next few pages, we will be doing more activities like these. I will tell you which question and row to work on. Then, without my help, you will mark under the correct answer. Do the best that you can with each question and do not worry if you are not sure of all of the answers. Be sure to bubble in the whole answer space each time you mark your answer. If you want to change an answer, erase all of your first mark and mark the new answer.

SAY: Look at the first row on the next page.

25. Listen carefully. Mark under the picture that shows two letters, two shapes, and three numbers.

26. Move down to the next row. Isaac's hardwood floor is dirty. He went to the store and bought several items to clean his floor. Mark under the picture that shows one of the items Isaac bought at the store.

27. Move down to the last row. Sasha wants to have a total of sixteen flowers in order to make a bouquet. At the beginning of the row, you can see the number of flowers that Sasha has already picked. Mark under the picture that shows the number of flowers she still needs to pick in order to make her bouquet.

SAY: Turn to the next page and look at the first row.

28. Maria went into her kitchen and heated up a pot of soup on the stove. Then, she poured the soup into a bowl and went to pick out a utensil from the drawer. Mark under the utensil that Maria took out of the drawer.

29. Look at the next row. Mark under the picture that shows an arrow pointing to a black triangle that is on top of a white circle.

30. Look at the bottom row. The figures in the boxes go together in a certain way as you move from left to right. Look at the figures to the right of the boxes. Mark under the figure that belongs in the empty box.

SAY: Look at the first row on the next page.

31. Mark under the picture that shows this: A car, a truck, and a bus are driving on a three-lane highway.

32. Move down to the next row. At the beginning of the row, you can see Johnny's allowance. Yesterday, he spent half of his allowance on candy. Mark under the picture that shows how much money Johnny has left.

INSTRUCTIONS

33. Move down to the last row. There was a terrible thunderstorm last night and lightning struck a tree in Brian's backyard. When Brian woke up this morning, he immediately looked out his bedroom window to see his backyard. Mark under the picture that shows what Brian saw.

SAY: Turn to the next page and look at the first row.

34. Sophie went to a family barbecue and sat in between her aunt and her grandfather. Since she was not feeling hungry, she only ate a few rolls of bread at the barbecue. Mark under the picture that shows Sophie sitting at her family barbecue.

35. Look at the next row. Mark under the picture that shows this: Alex has placed a pair of scissors, a bottle of glue, and a pencil on his table; the pencil is next to the scissors and the scissors are next to the bottle of glue.

36. Move down to the last row. Look at the row of shapes at the beginning of the row. Mark under the picture that shows how the shapes would look if the first shape became the third shape and the fourth shape became the second shape.

SAY: Look at the first row on the next page.

37. The figures inside the boxes go together in a certain way as you move from left to right. Look at the figures to the right of the boxes. Mark under the figure that belongs in the empty box.

38. Move down to the next row. Listen carefully. The hearts are doots, the spades are zonkers, and the diamonds are worleytots. Mark under the picture that shows the following order: worleytot, doot, worleytot, zonker.

39. Look at the bottom row. The figures in the boxes go together in a certain way as you move from left to right. Look at the group of figures to the right of the boxes. Mark under the figure that belongs in the empty box.

SAY: Stop working and put your pencil down. We will now take a break.

Administer a five-minute break. Make sure to tell the child that the test is not finished and that this is just a brief break.

INSTRUCTIONS

Part 3 (continued)

Tell the child that it is time to come back and continue with the activities.

SAY: **Turn to the next page and look at the first row.**

40. **Beth and Caitlin were heading out when Caitlin stopped Beth, handed her something, and said, "I think you should put this on because it is very windy outside." Mark under the item that Caitlin handed to Beth.**

41. **Move down to the next row. Mark under the picture that shows this: A man is fishing on a boat while a speedboat passes by pulling a woman on water skis.**

42. **Move down to the last row. Mark under the picture that shows this: There are three times as many puppies as there are eagles.**

SAY: **Look at the first row on the next page.**

43. **Tamara and Regina bought some chalk and drew some squares on the ground. Mark under the picture that shows what Tamara and Regina did next.**

44. **Look at the next row. The figures inside the boxes go together in a certain way as you move from left to right. Look at the figures to the right of the boxes. Mark under the figure that belongs in the empty box.**

45. **Look at the last row. Mark under the picture that shows a rectangle sitting on top of a triangle that is sitting on top of a circle.**

SAY: **Turn to the next page and look at the first row.**

46. **Dan and Carl went to a diner to eat breakfast. Dan ordered bacon and eggs and Carl ordered three pancakes. Both of them had a glass of orange juice with their breakfast. Dan finished his plate but Carl only ate half of his plate. However, Carl drank all of his orange juice while Dan only drank half of his orange juice. Mark under the picture that shows what the table looked like after Dan and Carl left the diner.**

47. **Move down to the next row. At the beginning of the row, you can see boxes of popcorn and drinks. Mark under the picture that shows the number of drinks that are needed so that there are an equal number of boxes of popcorn and drinks.**

48. **Move down to the last row. Amira went to the beach last weekend and built a small sandcastle close to the water at low tide. Mark under the picture that shows what Amira will see when she returns to the same place at the beach the next day.**

INSTRUCTIONS

SAY: Look at the first row on the next page.

49. Mark under the picture that shows a black star, a shaded square, a white diamond, and three different letters.

50. Look at the next row. Mark under the picture that has two small shapes inside of a larger shape.

51. Look at the last row. Greg does not like to eat things that taste sour. Mark under the picture that shows a type of food that Greg does not like to eat.

SAY: Turn to the next page and look at the first row.

52. The figures in the boxes go together in a certain way as you move from left to right. Look at the group of figures to the right of the boxes. Mark under the figure that belongs in the empty box.

53. Move down to the next row. Naomi went to the grocery store and bought eggs, butter, sugar, milk, flour, and chocolate icing. Then, she came home and used these ingredients to prepare a certain kind of food. Mark under the picture that shows what Naomi baked.

54. Move down to the last row. Mark under the picture that shows this: There are half as many napkins as plates.

SAY: Look at the first row on the next page.

55. Carrie took a piece of blank paper and drew a heart in the upper right-hand corner, the number "5" in the lower left-hand corner, and a stick figure in the middle of the paper. Mark under the picture that shows Carrie's piece of paper.

56. Look at the next row. Brandon is traveling to Hawaii in a few weeks. While he's there, he wants to go snorkeling. He already has a snorkel, but he also needs something for his feet. Mark under the item that Brandon needs to go snorkeling.

57. Look at the last row. The figures inside the boxes go together in a certain way as you move from left to right. Look at the figures to the right of the boxes. Mark under the figure that belongs in the empty box.

SAY: Turn to the next page and look at the first row.

58. Listen carefully. Linda wants to use numbers to represent letters. The number "4" is the letter "T", the number "2" is the letter "P", the number "6" is the letter "O', and the number 1 is the letter "S". Linda wrote down on a piece of paper, from left to right, the numbers "2", "6", "4", and "1". Mark under the picture that shows the word that is created by Linda's numbers.

INSTRUCTIONS

59. Move down to the next row. Leona owns four chairs and she wants to own a total of thirteen chairs. Mark under the picture that shows the number of chairs Leona needs to buy if she wants to own thirteen chairs.

60. Gary and Joseph were heading out to play baseball in the park when they heard a booming noise. Joseph looked out the window and said, "Well, I guess the game is going to be postponed." Mark under the picture that shows what Joseph saw when he looked out the window.

SAY: **We are now done with these activities for today. You may close your booklet now.**

Be sure to congratulate your child after he or she completes the test. Gather up the Student Booklet and the instructions. Grade the test on your own. Make sure to note the types of questions that your child found difficult to answer in order to determine possible problem areas. You should also wait for a day or two before you go over the practice test with your child.

ANSWER KEY

	Correct Answer	Student's Answer	Type of Question
1.	4		Picture Classification
2.	2		Figural Classification
3.	3		Figural Classification
4.	2		Picture Classification
5.	5		Figural Classification
6.	5		Picture Classification
7.	4		Figural Classification
8.	1		Figural Classification
9.	1		Picture Classification
10.	3		Figural Classification
11.	3		Picture Classification
12.	2		Figural Classification
13.	1		Picture Analogies
14.	2		Figural Analogies
15.	4		Figural Analogies
16.	3		Picture Analogies
17.	4		Figural Analogies
18.	3		Figural Analogies
19.	4		Picture Analogies
20.	1		Figural Analogies

ANSWER KEY

	Correct Answer	Student's Answer	Type of Question
21.	3		Figural Analogies
22.	2		Picture Analogies
23.	4		Picture Analogies
24.	1		Figural Analogies
25.	3		Following Directions
26.	4		Aural Reasoning
27.	1		Arithmetic Reasoning
28.	2		Aural Reasoning
29.	4		Following Directions
30.	2		Figural Series
31.	1		Following Directions
32.	3		Arithmetic Reasoning
33.	1		Aural Reasoning
34.	3		Aural Reasoning
35.	4		Following Directions
36.	2		Following Directions
37.	3		Pattern Matrix
38.	4		Following Directions
39.	3		Figural Series
40.	2		Aural Reasoning

ANSWER KEY

	Correct Answer	Student's Answer	Type of Question
41.	3		Following Directions
42.	4		Arithmetic Reasoning
43.	4		Aural Reasoning
44.	4		Pattern Matrix
45.	2		Following Directions
46.	3		Aural Reasoning
47.	4		Arithmetic Reasoning
48.	4		Aural Reasoning
49.	2		Following Directions
50.	3		Following Directions
51.	2		Aural Reasoning
52.	1		Figural Series
53.	1		Aural Reasoning
54.	3		Arithmetic Reasoning
55.	1		Following Directions
56.	1		Aural Reasoning
57.	2		Pattern Matrix
58.	3		Following Directions
59.	2		Arithmetic Reasoning
60.	3		Aural Reasoning

Bright Kids NYC OLSAT® Practice Test

Student's Booklet

Level C

Second Grade

STUDENT'S BOOKLET

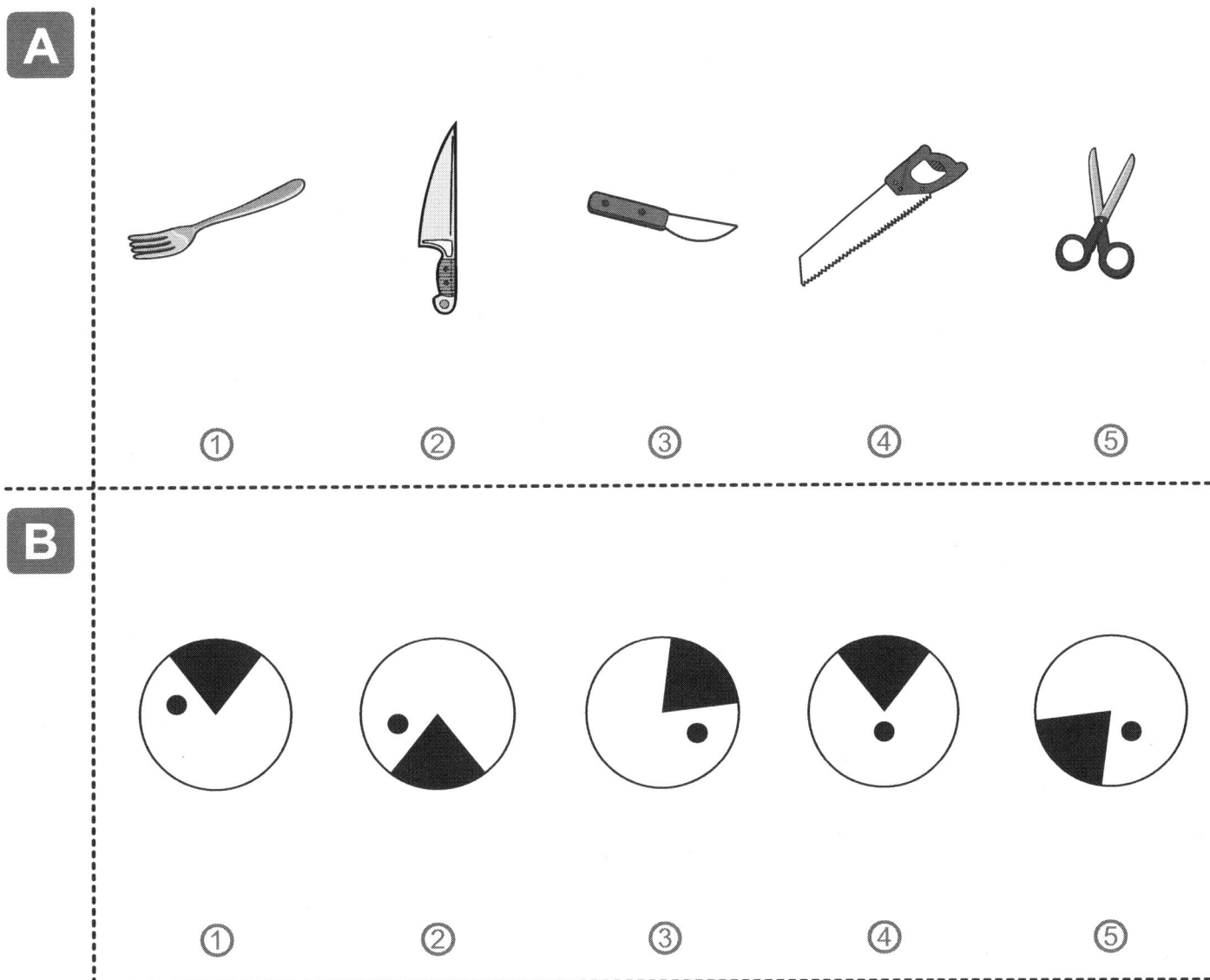

STUDENT'S BOOKLET

01

① ② ③ ④ ⑤

02

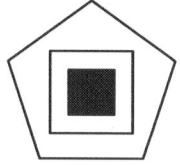 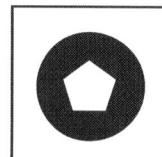 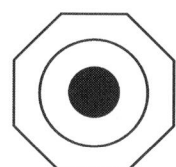  

① ② ③ ④ ⑤

03

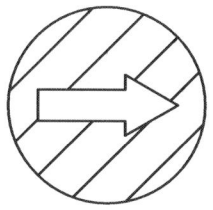 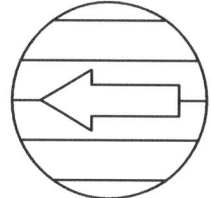 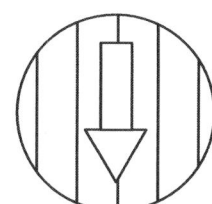 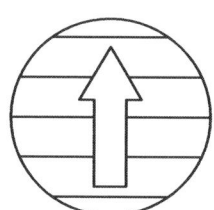 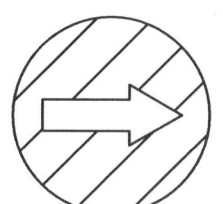

① ② ③ ④ ⑤

04

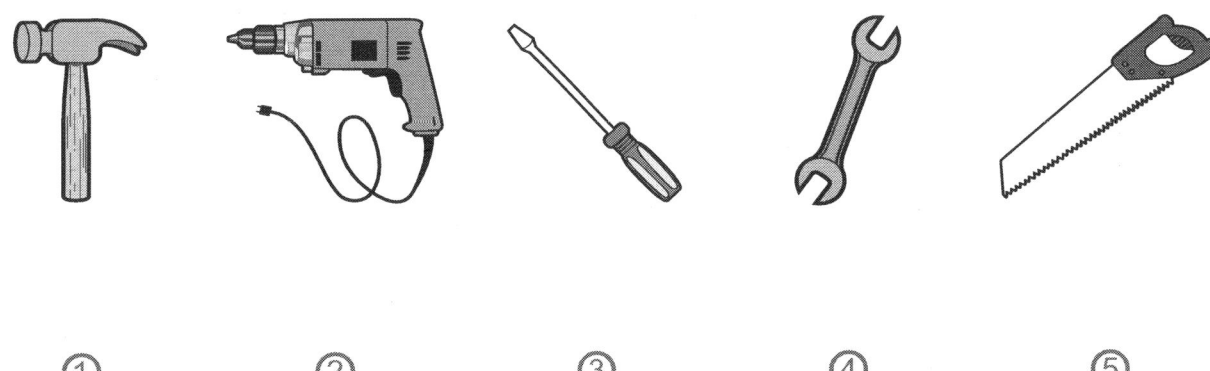

① ② ③ ④ ⑤

05

BCD   RST   KLM   HIJ   ZYX

① ② ③ ④ ⑤

06

  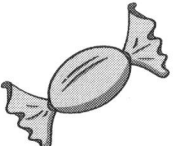  

① ② ③ ④ ⑤

STUDENT'S BOOKLET

07

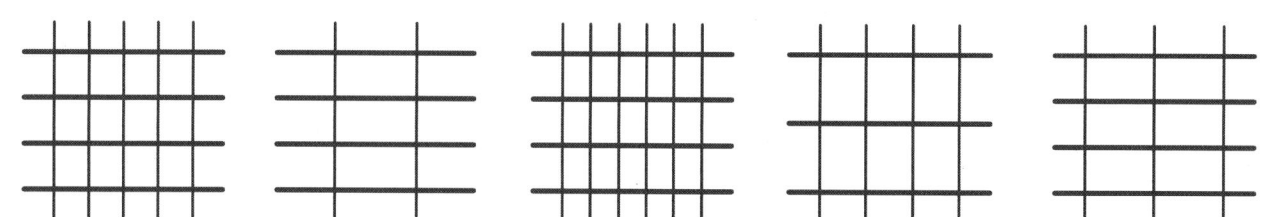

① ② ③ ④ ⑤

08

 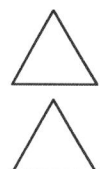 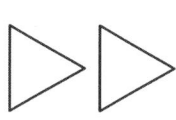 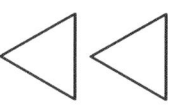 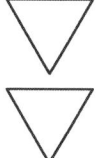

① ② ③ ④ ⑤

09

① ② ③ ④ ⑤

10

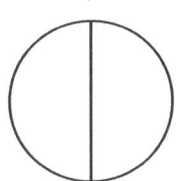 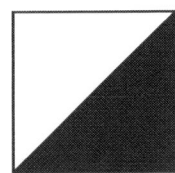 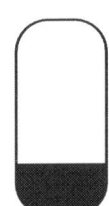 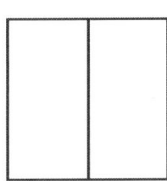 

① ② ③ ④ ⑤

11

① ② ③ ④ ⑤

12

 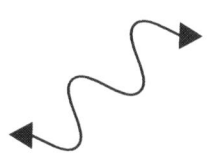 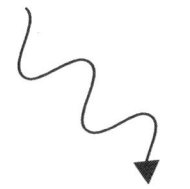 

① ② ③ ④ ⑤

STUDENT'S BOOKLET

C

① ② ③ ④

D

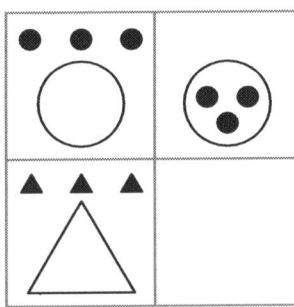    

① ② ③ ④

STUDENT'S BOOKLET

13

① ② ③ ④

14

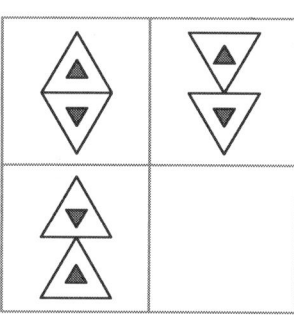    

① ② ③ ④

15

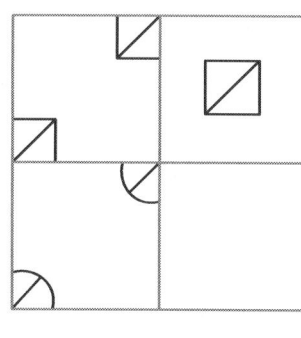

① ② ③ ④

STUDENT'S BOOKLET

16

 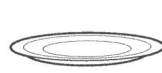   

① ② ③ ④

17

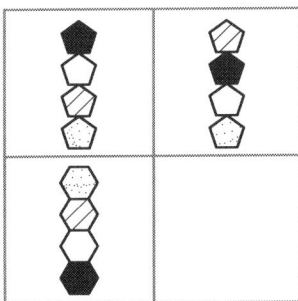    

① ② ③ ④

18

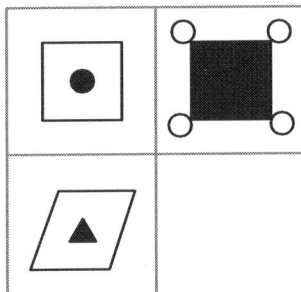  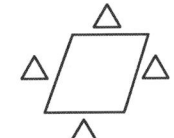  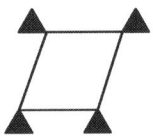

① ② ③ ④

Bright Kids NYC Inc. ©   OLSAT® Practice Test - Level C   51

STUDENT'S BOOKLET

19

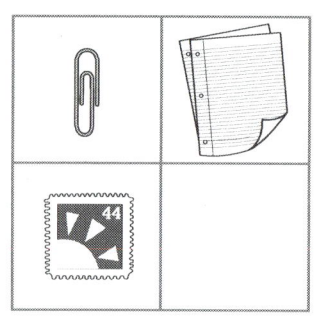    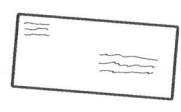

① ② ③ ④

20

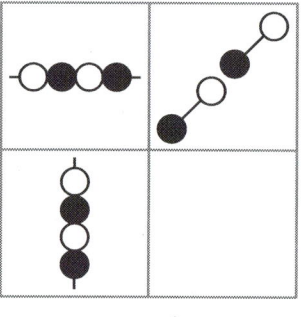 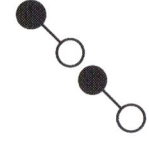  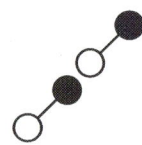 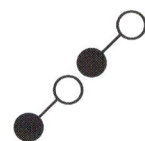

① ② ③ ④

21

① ② ③ ④

22

① ② ③ ④

23

① ② ③ ④

24

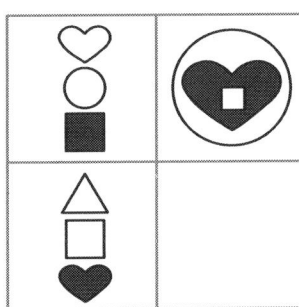    

① ② ③ ④

① ② ③ ④

 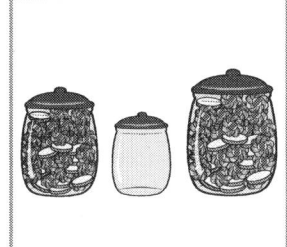  

① ② ③ ④

STUDENT'S BOOKLET

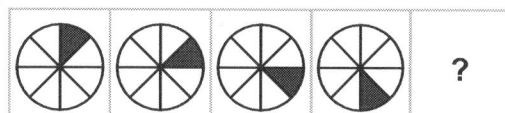      

① ② ③ ④

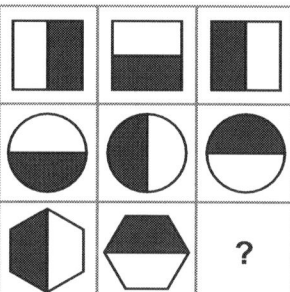

① ② ③ ④

25

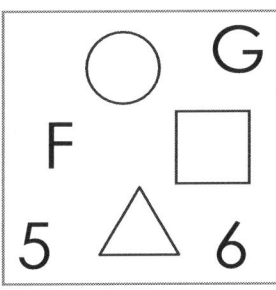 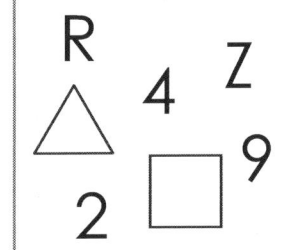 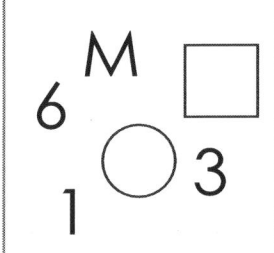

① ② ③ ④

26

  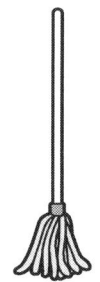

① ② ③ ④

27

① ② ③ ④

STUDENT'S BOOKLET

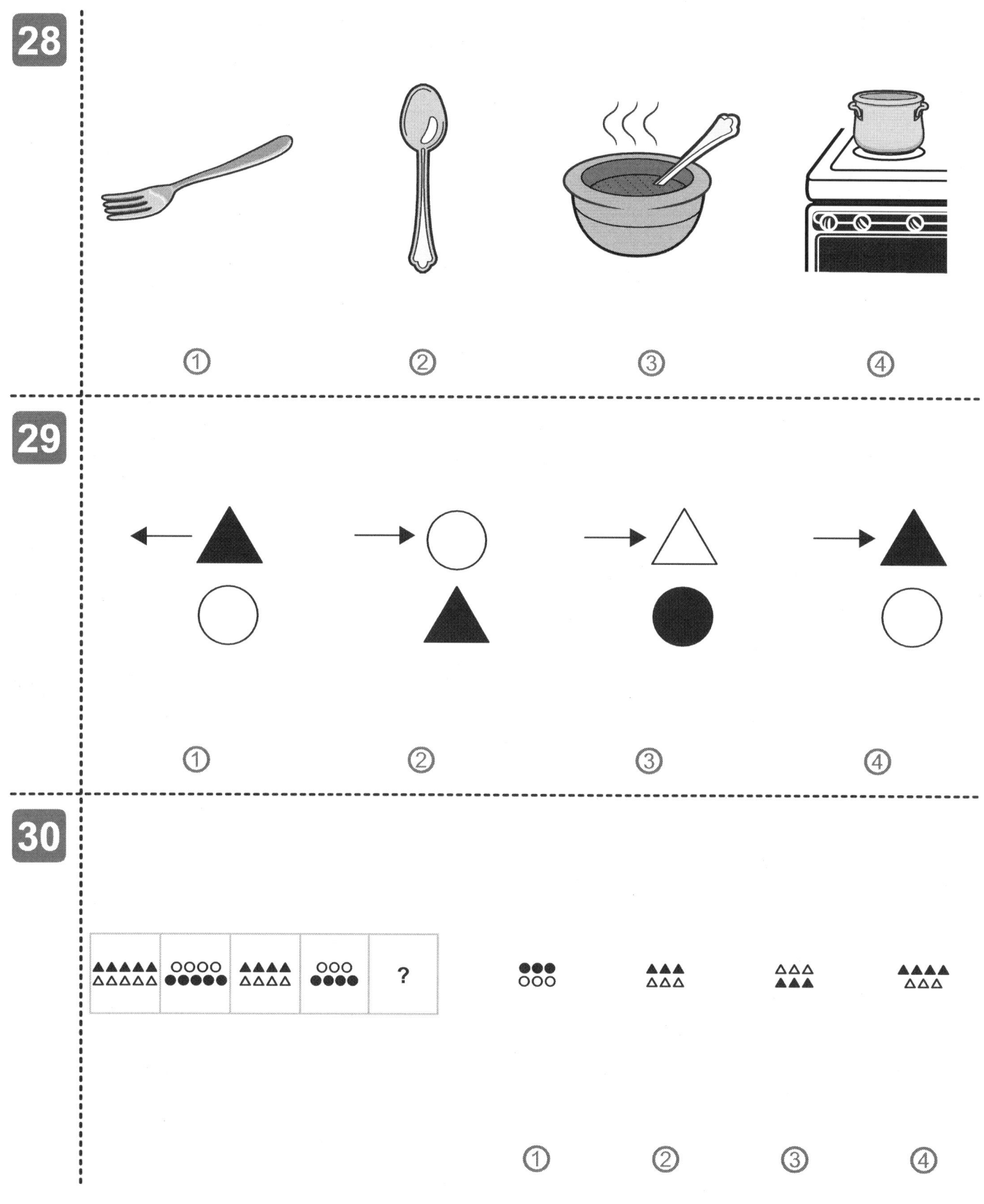

31

① ② ③ ④

32

 |

① ② ③ ④

33

① ② ③ ④

STUDENT'S BOOKLET

34

① ② ③ ④

35

 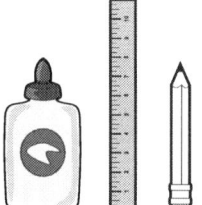 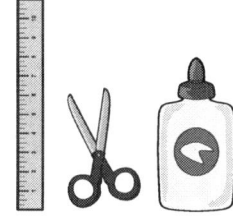 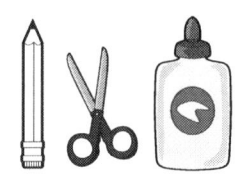

① ② ③ ④

36

 |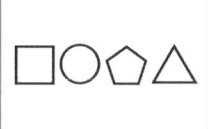

① ② ③ ④

37

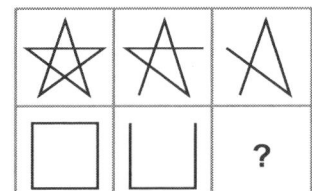   

① ② ③ ④

38

 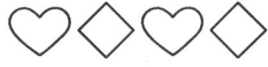  

① ② ③ ④

39

 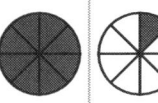 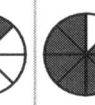

① ② ③ ④

STUDENT'S BOOKLET

40

① ② ③ ④

41

① ② ③ ④

42

① ② ③ ④

43

① ② ③ ④

44

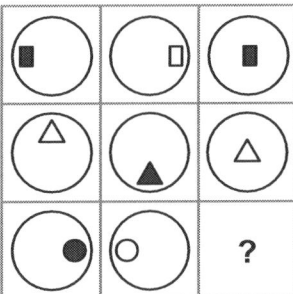

① ② ③ ④

45

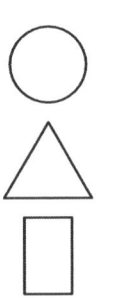   ②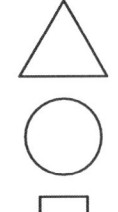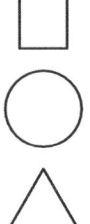

① ② ③ ④

STUDENT'S BOOKLET

46

   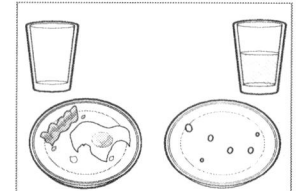

① ② ③ ④

47

① ② ③ ④

48

① ② ③ ④

49

① ② ③ ④

50

  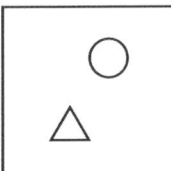 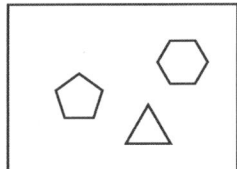

① ② ③ ④

51

① ② ③ ④

STUDENT'S BOOKLET

52

① ② ③ ④

53

 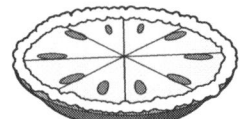  

① ② ③ ④

54

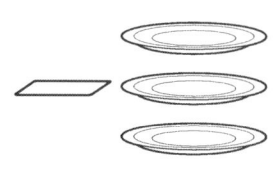  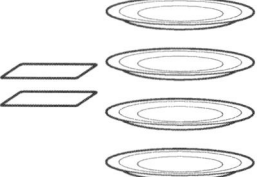 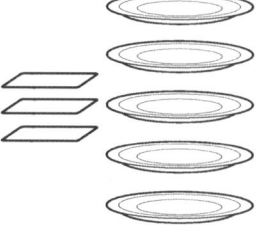

① ② ③ ④

55

① ② ③ ④

56

  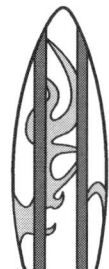 

① ② ③ ④

57

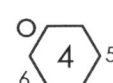 

① ② ③ ④

STUDENT'S BOOKLET

58

STOP	TOPS	POTS	POST
①	②	③	④

59

① ② ③ ④

60

 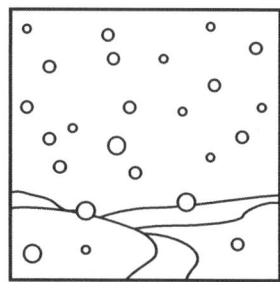  

① ② ③ ④